The Wizard Of Id
My Kingdom
For A Horsie!

Johnny Hart &
Brant Parker

CORONET BOOKS
Hodder and Stoughton

Copyright © 1976 by Field Newspaper Syndicate.

First published in the United States of
America by Ballantine Books in 1984.

Coronet edition 1985

British Library C.I.P.

Hart, Johnny
    The wizard of Id, my kingdom for a horsie!
    I. Title   II. Parker, Brant
    813'.54]F]   PS3557.A/

    ISBN 0 340 37191 9

Printed and bound in Great Britain for
Hodder and Stoughton Paperbacks, a
division of Hodder and Stoughton Ltd.,
Mill Road, Dunton Green, Sevenoaks,
Kent (Editorial Office: 47 Bedford
Square, London, WC1 3DP) by
Hunt Barnard Printing Ltd.,
Aylesbury, Bucks.

GLUG
GLUG
GLUG
GLUG
GLUG
GLUG

WE ARE TRYING THIS MAN BY THE ANCIENT "SALIVA JURY" TECHNIQUE.

... WE PLACE PEBBLES IN HIS MOUTH, THEN READ HIS CRIMES ALOUD...

3-1

..IF THE PEBBLES ARE WET... HE'S INNOCENT... DRY, HE'S GUILTY.

WHAT IF HE SWALLOWS THEM?

HE'S HUNGRY.

3-8

3-10

3·12

3-18

3·19

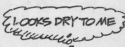

LOOKS DRY TO ME

3-20

4-1

WHAT'S THE CHEAPEST CASKET YOU CAN BUY?

THIS CORRUGATED CARDBOARD JOB GOES FOR $12.98

I'LL TAKE IT!

4.9

WHERE DO YOU WANT THE BODY MAILED?

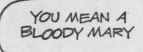

4-22

I'M TAKING CUDDLES TO THE VET...

HE NEEDS HIS SHOTS... HIS NAILS NEED CLIPPING... HIS VITAMINS ARE OVERDUE... HIS EARS NEED CLEANING ...HIS HAIR IS DIRTY AND HE'S BEEN OFF HIS FEED

4-27

WHY DON'T YOU TAKE GRANDPA TOO?

4.29

4-30

5-5

5-6

WHO ARE YOU GOING TO APPOINT AS THE NEW AMBASSADOR, SIRE?

I DON'T KNOW.... BUT I'D SURE LIKE TO HAVE A "MAN OF LETTERS"

GOT JUST THE GUY, SIRE

5-8

WHO'S THIS?

STANLEY KLUTZ... THE INVENTOR OF ALPHABET SOUP

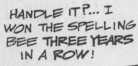

6-2

68

6·15

6·17

SIRE!

...UH... I... SUPPOSE THE DOCTOR LIVINGSTONE ROUTINE WOULD BE A WASTE OF TIME?......

7·3

7-6

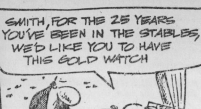

7·16

I BOUGHT NEW CLUBS WITH A STIFF SHAFT

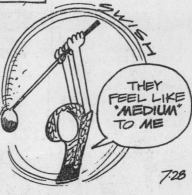

THEY FEEL LIKE "MEDIUM" TO ME

7-28

THEY CHARGED ME 900 DOLLARS

...THAT'S A STIFF SHAFT